HEART NOTES

Caleb "The Negro Artist" Rainey

Copyright © 2019 Caleb Rainey

All rights reserved. This book or any portion thereof may not be reproduced or used in any manner whatsoever without the express written permission of the publisher except for the use of brief quotations in a book review.

Cover design by Ophelia Flores-Carr.

First edition, 2019

thenegroartist.com
Facebook.com/thenegroartist
Instagram.com/the_negroartist

ISBN:
9781695282629

To everyone who dares to love.

CONTENTS

PART ONE

Love Easy	1
The Coward	5
In Silence	6
To the Girl Who Wants to be a Poem	8
Writing Time	10
Caveman	13
In the Next Town Over	14
Ride	16
Buried	17
Back Together	19
Heart Surgery	21
Mortgage Dreams	23
February 13th	24
Own	25
Rubik's Cube	26
The Path Not Taken	29
What You Need to Hear	30

HEART NOTES

PART TWO

Discovery	35
Lottery	37
A Simple Love Poem	39
Look	41
Tattoos & Sex Shops	43
My Love is a Traveler	45
The Unknown Continent	46
Wendy the Good Little Witch	47
The Light	49
Desperaux	50
Parting Gift	52
Spring	54
Bright	56
Ritual	57
On Staying	59
Ghost Ships	60
Bubble Tea Haiku	61
Eden	62
What a Beautiful World	64

HEART NOTES

PART ONE

HEART NOTES

LOVE EASY

My mother said as a child I'd walk
through the park, run up to
the unsuspecting man on the bench
and sit on his lap.
While waiting in line at the Wal-Mart register
I'd make friends with the cashier.
In the mall I'd start a game of tag
with kids I'd never met.

As a child
I loved people.
I savored each smile,
the way the shape of your lips
lifted your face meant the world
wasn't so heavy. To laugh was
like washing your spirit
to hold hands and hug,
to kiss and cuddle,
was like touching truth.

My mother said I was a dangerous child
because I loved too easy.

I used to wear my heart on my sleeve
but it fell into the wrong hands
and then parted like the red sea
and she tore my heart into pieces.
Now, I've forgotten what it means
to love easy.

HEART NOTES

Now, I love to ask people questions.
During conversations I accurately calculate
ways to keep you chatting because it's safer
to ask questions than to answer them.

Now, when I crash down onto my bed,
I like to find the corners of my blanket
so I know where comfort ends.

Now, I love Taco Bell burritos
but I never eat the last bite.
I fold the wrapper like a baby's blanket
and hold my bundle of joy finally
getting to love something
that isn't swallowed up whole.

Now, I only write with pens
convinced that my mistakes be permanent.
The page is my body
and with each word crossed out
I gain a new scar across my skin.

Now, I love hot wings.
I have always loved hot wings
but now, it is safe.
I can eat 25
in 1 sitting
only getting sauce on 2 fingers.
I found a way to substitute mess with system.
I'm not sure if I've mastered the art of loving
or if I'm just scared of messy love.

HEART NOTES

I don't think I was supposed to be this way,
each day pushing away
from people and pain.
That's not what life's supposed to teach
so I reach
        I reach
                I reach
                      for reminders.

Remember to listen to music.
Even though I can never remember
lyrics to songs, I'm reminded of how
the rhythm of the words bounce through my ears,
down my bones, and into my being.
This is true love, because
I accept them for who they are
and do not try to tame them.

Remember to solve more puzzles
because they remind me that pieces
can still come together to make magnificent art.

Remember to collect more playing cards
to remind myself that life's a deck,
and there's still a queen of hearts somewhere,
you just have to pray for a good shuffle.

Remember to play with kids
because they remind me of what the key to life is
since they haven't lost theirs yet.
It's not systems   it's not selfishness   it's not security

HEART NOTES

It's simple:
love easy

THE COWARD

You walk towards me / and when my mind registers / who you are, I decide then and there / I am going to love you. / Fiercely. / You are a gazelle / and I want to devour you. / The way your body sways makes me want / to be a traveler trying to find his way / along your curves. / You walk towards me. / You expose that involuntary smile / I decide then and there / I am going to love you. / Passionately. / Be the blood to my heart / this pumping meaning nothing / without you. / I will forever work to keep you / smiling, so the world can admire you / like the Mona Lisa / so the world can admire you like I do. / You walk towards me. / I smile with a joy that can only be / matched when love is genuine. / Before you're close enough / for me to tell you what I've decided, / my phone rings. / I look down. / It's my girlfriend. / I hold the phone gingerly, cold metal in sweaty palm / I look up to see you / standing next to me and I decide right then and there / I am a coward. "I have to take this," I say / as I turn my back to you and walk away.

IN SILENCE

She told me relationships were
overrated, none of the ones she'd ever seen ever made it.
She didn't need one, they're more deadly than a gun.
She told me that she would rather have an F.W.B.
then she could make love with no strings
both getting what they want but never what they need,
only dependency was on the dirty deed
and she said she saw nothing wrong with that.
And I sat in silence.

She told me that she secretly wished she was a virgin,
she had lost herself somewhere she had never been.
She could tell part of herself was gone,
never knew love and sex were such cons.
He said all the right words at the right time
and like a lullaby she fell for every line
dreaming of fantasies and fairy tales
thinking love could never fail.
She thought he knew what she didn't,
let herself forget what God had written.
She did what they all said to do
but in the end she didn't feel like she was supposed to.
Now she has come to terms with the fact that men take,
and she's going to keep making mistakes
and she said she saw nothing wrong with that.
And I sat in silence.

She told me that she didn't want to be extraordinary,
her life goal was to be extra-ordinary,
being normal was safe in a world full of hate.

HEART NOTES

She asked, if you lost her in the crowd,
how would you be able to put her down?
She said she realized that popularity was in fact,
a target on her back, that caused other girls
to send her in into exile, while boys judged her,
beauty pageant style.
She said she wanted me to look at her and
gain no impression, because she knew
she wouldn't be able to live up to the expectations
and she said she saw nothing wrong with that.
                    I sat in silence
                    you sat in silence
                    we sat in silence

Instead of telling her what she needed to hear.
Not everything ends in tears.
We should have said that healthy relationships make
healthy lives, and that it's impossible to do
anything without making emotional ties.
We should have said she could wait
on having S.E.X. because in love is when it's the best.
We should have told her that she could save herself
for the right one
instead of doing what everyone else has done.
We should have told her that
being extraordinary isn't a curse,
being like everyone else is worse.
We should have told her that God made the sun to shine
and with her, He had the same thing in mind.
We should have told her that. But

We sat in silence.

HEART NOTES

TO THE GIRL WHO WANTS TO BE A POEM

You think your body is
meant to be metaphor broken
into bits, scattered across pages,
irresponsible poets play with you.

You look in the mirror
and see your smile as a simile,
remembering you are only
      Like
like beautiful
like appreciated
like loved
stuck wondering what it feels like to
Be.

Your lungs are relentless
repetition. Each breath
a memory of moments
the sun cannot reach
and darkness calls home.

You put your hand to your heart
and think the rhythm is
the sound of breaking.

Every time I meet you I want
to write you into a Band-Aid.
I urge my words to wrap you
in warmth so hot it does not burn
but simply melts all

HEART NOTES

the lies off your skin.

I pray my voice can carry
your insecurities and drop them
off a cliff so you can see
how they hold you down.

I hope my hands can move
mountains of bad memories
and flatten them into valleys of value,
overflowing with worth.

I throw my heart
at you and beg you
stay above water
hold on tight

I want to be the poet that saves you
but you are not a poem,
and I am not a god.

WRITING TIME

FALL 2002
AGE 7
After hating writing
because it is both hard and riddled
with restricting prompts
I learn to really read,
and I find I can create my own rules.

WINTER 2006
AGE 11
Direct quote:
"Poetry is just another way to express
our feelings, but more difficult.
I think poetry is the *most boring* thing to write,
but good poetry is not all that bad to read.
I also think that when I'm older, most likely,
I will write poetry."

FALL 2010
AGE 15
I write my first love poem.
I feel inspired in a way
I never could have imagined.
We've been together for a month and I am sure
this is true love. My pen cannot keep up
with the pitter patter of my heart.

WINTER 2010
AGE 15
It's the night before my birthday

and I write a prayer to God, asking
that her period comes
before I turn 16.

SPRING 2011
AGE 16
I will not pick up a pen.
I will not write again.
Baby and dead
should never be in the same sentence.

SPRING 2012
AGE 17
I am lonely.
Empty.
A pencil without lead, moving
without purpose. I write
a poem to impress a girl.
It works.

FALL 2012
AGE 17
I am friends with feelings again,
but only the ones I can tame with a #2 pencil.
I am single again and I still can't
figure out how to fit
love in between the lines
but I write now, and right now,
that's better than where I was.

SPRING 2013
AGE 18

HEART NOTES

I write my first love poem again.
Valentine's Day is tomorrow
and though we are new
and it is not yet love,
I can see space for it again
      in the margins
spilling over to the second page.
I am looking forward.

CAVEMAN

I was your caveman,
artist with fingertips to stone,
we were making history our own.

We started young but
our friendship felt old,
like something lost and found
ancient and lasting
we knew each other
better than we knew ourselves.

Maybe that was the problem,
it's hard to love and be loved
before we know who we are
and I was only a caveman,
a Neanderthal, an infant
in the ways it really mattered.

I could make art but not complete
the picture. Too many pieces
yet to be uncovered and
I still needed to evolve.
Time offers the growth
internally and individually.
and that means we could
not dwell together, but
our writing is still on the walls.

I hope someone else finds
the proof of our presence.

HEART NOTES

IN THE NEXT TOWN OVER

We pretended to be different
like we are in love and not afraid
to show it. Hold hands
while weaving through
strangers on sidewalks. We share
smiles. We pretend

we have never been a secret, simply
never in the right place
or the right time. This is
our time, in a town where no one knows
us or the lies we've told
to tie each other together.

You ask if we'd be happy,
which is to ask, is there a world
where we work and it's real and
there's no hiding. My vocal cords knot,
not sure how to untangle the truth.

                                                         Yes
                                        Yes
                              Yes
                      Yes
              Yes
Yes
unravels between us.
Your heart tugs at mine and
the tension is taut in my chest.
You are tired of being a loose end
but I don't know how to

HEART NOTES

cut you off or make ends meet.

Eventually, on the way home
our interwoven fingers will split, you
will realize I am more rope burn than safety net
no amount of time and love and hope can fix
a tangled heart and you will lace up yours,
walk to another town and call it your own.

RIDE

We were stuck
on a carousel, circling
the same fights
pointing at the same
beasts we'd never able to tame.
A lion's share of trust issues
and zebra stripes of right and wrong.
We were animals
in our own right
tore into each other with
ferocious fear and
instinctual insecurity
around and around we went
until we got dizzy and
neither of us know why
we were on the same ride.

BURIED

What makes it hard to get out
of bed after   a break up   is not
only the weight of the word why
        but that your bed never asks
for anything but a body

lay limp   eyes casket closed   stiff sleep

This is the closest I can be to
dead, some days I feel
like I should stay that way.

TAKE CARE

I know you **have been hurt** by someone else, can tell by the way you **carry** yourself. If you'll let **me**, here's what I'll do, I'll take care of you. You hate being **alone**, well you ain't the only one. You **hate** the fact that you bought **the dream** and they sold you one. **Now** I'm dealing with **a heart** I didn't **break**. If you'll let me, here's what I'll do, **I**'ll take care of you. You won't ever have to **worry**, you **won't ever** have to hurt. I'll **be** there for you, I will care of you, I keep thinking you just don't know. Trying to run from that, saying you're **done** with that, on your face boy it just don't show. When you're ready, just say you're ready.

If you'll let me, here's what I'll do, I'll take care of you.

BACK TOGETHER

I remember the Monday you decided you didn't need me. The Monday you realized you didn't want me. The Monday you put the magnifying glass to our relationship. You said you were trying to look closer but like any sadistic kid, you hoped to catch the sunlight. You wanted to watch us burn.

The space between your words reminds me too much of the emptiness you left in my heart when you decided your love needed a vacation a spring break from my affection. A walk on the beach of men, each a grain of sand wanting to stick to your body. Your body only partially covered by the vibrant two piece of insecurity & trust issues. Tanning in the light of maybes, so sun rays like *maybe I don't want a relationship* or *maybe I'm not in love* start seeping into your skin and you begin to hope you get a tan. Dip toes in the ocean of possibilities without us, and find the water cold but refreshing.

Like all vacations, you came back. You came home.

While you were away this home was tearing itself down trying to rebuild itself into a house you'd want to live in. The kind of house you want to raise children in.

HEART NOTES

Now you're back but I'm afraid you bought a vacation house.

It's not that I hate him.
I do hate him.
I hate that his hands held your hope in them
his lips spoke your escape into existence
his height shows that your eyes were set on life above me.
He means your absence.
He means my absence.
He means your acceptance of my absence.
He is the face of my heartbreak
the face of the life you could have had
and at one point, truly wanted.
So maybe you don't want him anymore
but on days when I'm not easy to love
you'll think back to what he means and you'll consider it.

And that's why I get a panic attack every Sunday night.
My stomach hardens like concrete,
my lungs are twin towers that collapse onto my heart
my trembling hands hold my knee caps and wait
for the earthquake inside me to stop
my jaw open like the screen door someone forgot to shut
my throat is the front door to my heart, sealed
shut with too many deadbolts with missing keys
so I don't make a sound, swallowed up by my own silence
forced to watch Sunday set and Monday rise again.

HEART SURGERY

After my 5 & a half year relationship
I ask my best friend,
How do I move on?
He says,
You know how you'd reach in your closet,
grab a sweater, and there's one of her hairs on it?
        It's like that.
You have to remove all the loose strands.

Her hair was the first thing I noticed.
Marching on a high school football field
the summer heat seemed to come
from the fire flickering on her head.

Months later we'd curl up on a couch
I'd complain about her hairs clinging to
my clothes like an infant grips a finger.
She'd tell me it's a manifestation of her love.
It can't get enough of me.

Now I am a surgeon
each strand of hair
a heart string
I must sever.
I must hold the scalpel
with honest, steady hands
as I attempt to keep
the heart beating.

Last week I found her hair

HEART NOTES

on a pillow made out of our first
marching band uniform.
I pull it from the thread and in my head
I can't ignore the proposal I'd planned.
Her ring size still written
as a reminder in my phone.
I had the marching band on standby,
with a football field full of future plans.
How do you remove a memory of
something that never happened,
only ever imagined?

When I walk through my place
her hair curls from the carpet
and catches my toes.
I discover a new kind of cardiac arrest.

How do I orchestrate
my own open heart surgery?

       It is essential.

It's either successfully snip every strand,
or flat-line on failed futures.
This surgery seems hungry for a funeral,
and I'm not always sure
what's meant to be buried,
my body or my broken
but I know that hurting
and healing are more siblings
than enemies,
and that faith is in the same family.

MORTGAGE DREAMS

The problem is I already called you wife.
Welcomed the word into fantasy
walk through the front door
kick off your shoes, stay awhile.

The problem is I already built a home for
you in my heart, so when we went shopping for
real homes, discussing loans and interest rates
I didn't expect your interest to decline.
> We already lived together in my world.
> I thought it was our world.

The problem is I always feel too
big, love too big, dream too big.
That must be why you were afraid to wake me. Maybe
I was born a sleepwalker because the path we were on felt
so natural. I don't know where
I'd be if you hadn't woken me
probably somewhere happy.

But in this reality, we did not buy that house.

Instead, 2 months later I have a new couch
in my apartment that I can't get comfortable on
and the police find squatters living in that house
with chairs under doorknobs and blankets over windows
they had bright ideas on how to build happiness.
Maybe they were like me, maybe they were dreamers too.
But the problem is reality is always darker than the dreams.

FEBRUARY 13TH: AN ANNIVERSARY

The bus is late.
I wait for
you to say something
that I know you won't.
The day has been loud and failing
to drown the silence.
We do not own today
like anyone else
we do not own each other.
All we hold are our memories
in the same hands
once ready to fold futures together
like fingers wedlock.

I could speak to
the space between us
but the bus comes,
the day ends.
I do not say a word.

OWN

There are things you still own like the word *babe* and
Friday night pizzas, they feel like they came from you,
our relationship the god of those creations and it feels
like blasphemy to give them to anyone else
but I don't know what to do when a god dies.

How do I fit two bodies and a future into one casket?
Does burying a god look like forgetting?
I don't remember how to do that
when you are everywhere, leading me
in the grocery store aisle or
baking soft cookies that melt
in your mouth. I dissolve
into dreams or memories or
the habit of loving. You seem to own
that too. Your sweet fingerprints
all over my heart and I don't want
to call you a thief, but I don't know
how to own my heart anymore.

HEART NOTES

RUBIK'S CUBE

Stolen moments on stairwells,
fingers fumbling with colors
we can't quite grasp yet.

Slide Right

White light laughter bouncing
off walls and building
a foundation, a home base for joy.
We may not know how to match
all the colors yet, but we know
we can always meet here.

Slide Right

There in the stairwell with
red rose petal passion when
hands touch and cheeks blush,
all that beauty blooming between them.

Slide Down

To the ground growing green with new
pieces being placed next to each other, like
patience and appreciation. They will grow and
deepen in time.

Slide Up, Slide Up

To ocean blue waves where we learn

HEART NOTES

rhythm and how some days our hands are
tired or lost or hopeless but we find
each other to hold onto.

Slide Left

To the side of tomorrow's sunrise,
we're putting together all this yellow hope
and we are so close.
We are looking forward and
seeing a brighter day.

Slide Down

To the orange spark, the last step.
Both technical and natural,
We would never find each other
In this stairwell if it weren't for this.
A mysterious warmth, there from the beginning
but grows as the colors come together.
When we solve the sides, sparks fly.

Slide Right

		Right			*Up*
Left			*Left*		
	Down			*Right*	
	Right				*Down*
Down		*Down*			
	Left		*Down*		

Year later I will wonder who
shuffled the first side.

HEART NOTES

Who's hand slipped and slid
up, down and around
our pattern turned puzzle
that our fingers forgot how to solve.
              I don't think it will matter.
All that will matter
is that we sat together,
hearts in hands, showing our sides
and tried to love with all the colors.

HEART NOTES

THE PATH NOT TAKEN

I have to tell myself
we're both happier this way.

                        Most days, it's easy.

I have a job that pays well,
a partner to lean on,
and friends that support me.

                        I think you have that too.

Then   there are days where I wonder
if your hair smells the same
        or if you still bite your nails like I do
                or if you still smoke cigarettes
                        or if you still write poems
                            about moments we cant change.

I wonder if you think of the hypotheticals.

                      Like, what if everything we wrote
                            became true? What if
        the happiness we wrote ourselves into
                          became reality? What if
I wasn't a coward? Our lives would be different
            now. Most days that I   travel
      down   this path I have to think

    we'd be happy that way too.

HEART NOTES

WHAT YOU NEED TO HEAR

1.
You matter.
I know some days you feel like a spider,
a lone weaver, sowing life together on your own
and there are days you only catch crap or worse, nothing.
You go to bed wondering if your web is only your coffin,
if you're even meant to be a spider.
I need to tell you
wait until   the morning dew
wait until   you see sunlight
reflect off bulbs of water
on strands you didn't even know were there.
Those are the strands that connect us
        connect you to me.
They're what holds us all together.
We need them.
We need you.
Your life is more
than you can see sometimes
so every night look at your web and await
the sunlight.

2.
You have power.
Everything tells you
you don't.
The media,
the police,
       the teachers,
             the bosses,

HEART NOTES

                        the mirror,
they say you can't control anything
that the history haunting you
the system shackled around your ankles
the trauma noose tight on your neck
is all you can think about.
It should direct your every step.
They're wrong.
You can make each moment
a rebellion, an I-dare-you dance
where you laugh at every chance,
trust at first glance, and smile in advance.
Lift the weight of oppression
by choosing connection.
Thwart trauma with truth telling.
Shatter systems with sincerity.
You can change lives
you simply have to   fight.

3.
We matter.
Trade your mirror
for a window and see
the beauty we all have to offer.

4.
You are not finished.
Who you are now is not
who you will be.
You are growing in God's garden
among us. We all bloom
in our own time.

HEART NOTES

We all bloom.
And soon, you
will flourish into the flower
that blooms brave,
petals soft and passionate,
colors vibrant.
You will be so spectacular
God stops to smell.

5.
I love you
                                  I love you
                 I love you
                                            I love you
I love you

HEART NOTES

PART TWO

HEART NOTES

DISCOVERY

You've always had good eyes and dedicated hands,
an archaeologist diligent and delicate
digging into people to bring out what is
buried and beautiful and begging to be seen.

Let me be your dirt.

MAGNET POEM 1/7

    Listen
your heart is a secret
safe with me always
    Feel
how hugs are
our home

LOTTERY

when you first tell someone
you love them and they say they love you too
        but they don't love you

You will know
or later you will think that you did.
You will remind yourself of how
there are people who think
they've won the lottery before
they hear the last number.

        You will be one of them.

You will find yourself in bed at 3am wondering
what you would have done with all those winnings
what that kind of happiness would look like
You're sure you would have done something good with it,
        like nurture it,
            help it grow.

You will toss and turn and find yourself
wondering who did win, how did they get so lucky?
You try your whole life to make it,
but you're still out of luck
and the next day
You will find yourself in line
waiting to get a ticket
wondering if you will play the same numbers.

HEART NOTES

MAGNET POEM 2/7

Listen to love
feel it flower
in you
beautiful
happiness

HEART NOTES

A SIMPLE LOVE POEM

I'm so in love I may need a doctor
after a fall like that.

I'm so in love every song on the radio reminds me of you
so in love clichés don't make me cringe anymore.

I'm so in love that if love were a house
I'd never leave,
just curl up on your soft-lip couch
next to your fireplace heart.

I'm so in love your mouth feels like a metaphor
the meeting of meaning and magic.

I'm so in love outer space seems smaller
than your smile, each of your teeth shining
like stars guiding me home.

I'm so in love I think of your milky way skin,
and want to explore it from end to end
but spend most of my time in the solar system of your
thoughts.

I'm so in love I think of your laugh when
I hear something funny,
like your joy and mine are twin suns
orbiting each other. Where one is,
the other is sure to be close.

I'm so in love that waking up to

HEART NOTES

see sunlight on your face
seems like a new kind of day dream.

I'm so in love that I find myself thinking about
flowers. I've never wanted to be a gardener,
afraid to love something that can't love me back
but now I dream about planting daffodils
so I can admire them dancing in daylight.

I'm so in love each day seems to bloom into a thank you.

I'm so in love smiling now seems
involuntary, like breathing
or joy.

I'm so in love I forgot
what a secret is.
So in love I'm learning
new words like warmth, trust, full.
So in love that whenever I learn something new
I want to share it with you.

I'm so in love
I want to share everything with you.
My food? Take it.
My words? Have them.
My heart? Don't drop it.

LOOK

She sees the world
the way it begs to be seen
big and b o u n d l e s s

      She knows
how to spot the beauty in
the places unknown to her.

      I hope
one day she looks into my eyes,
notices her reflection, and
realizes she's an unknown world.

I hope she sees the beauty.

MAGNET POEM 3/7

I know
the word happy
      your heart
shared its secret
      Listen
a beautiful feeling

TATTOOS & SEX SHOPS

We are today, and always,
attempting to make something permanent
out of pain and pleasure.

When you got the sun tattooed on your hand,
you smiled at the thought of holding such light.
I wondered if you realized that's the same
smile I have when my fingers find yours.

I traced Truth and Love across my wrists to insist
that you taught me the two things I have in this life,
and yes, Truth hurt more than love
but I extend both to you.

When we find our way into a sex shop you fidget with
excitement, nerves, and the knowledge that we are
alive right now.
Right now we are being the most human we can be
and we laugh because words can't contain us or joy or love
and we don't know the difference anymore.

We do not know what tomorrow holds,
but we know that today our bodies are ours
and by ours, we mean we each have two bodies or
have become one body or in the only way we know how
we have tied ourselves to time, to touch, to skin.

MAGNET POEM 4/7

words we share
a secret safe
in my heart
a home for us

   Always

MY LOVE IS A TRAVELER

My heart outside
my body. Wandering through
the world, deep and dangerous.
She never stays
too long. Searching for more.
Finds light in the little
bit of wild. We all have
something to share.
My love is
mine and yours.

THE UNKNOWN CONTINENT

You've never been to ~~love~~ Australia
but you are sure you want to go,
sure there is something there for you
~~my heart~~ the eucalyptus tree grows for you, hopes
that you will be a ~~romantic~~ koala that holds on tight
that finds peace, finds rest, finds home
in its ~~arms~~ branches.

HEART NOTES

WENDY THE GOOD LITTLE WITCH & CASPER THE FRIENDLY GHOST

Wendy loves the idea of empty
loves surrendering to space
looks in the mirror and tries to look through
sucks in her tummy in attempt to be transparent
hugs the toilet to rid herself of all this
matter of fact she sees Casper as a champion
both there and gone, invisible and felt

I keep falling in love with Wendy
a woman with all this magic inside her
she feels big to me
big like the sun,
casting out all the shadows in summer time
big like a library,
full of stories that conjure up compassion
big like the dinner table,
there's always room for one more

I want her to take up the space next to me.

But Casper keeps getting in the way
has got her chasing after him
focusing more on the word *little* than good
or maybe she slipped into a spell and
made them synonyms
it's got her disappearing before my eyes

I don't know how to love a ghost
don't know how to convince her

HEART NOTES

all her magic isn't a mistake
she's made full of fantasy
I couldn't dream bigger

I see her.
I love her.
The only kind of magic I can make.
Somewhere she lost that spell for herself
I try to share mine but Casper was here first and
the dead don't love the living but misery loves company
so when I see her, she is my favorite thing to see
and I hope my eyes remind her of who she really is.
Alive and Beautiful.

HEART NOTES

THE LIGHT

Sometimes
I call you a *delight*
but perhaps I mean *the light*,
which is to say I've seen sunrays
in your eyes, each blink a revolution
from night to day. I love when you
shine on me, a summertime smile
sneaks up on me. I hope it
never ends.

DESPERAUX

When I question why we have to end
whether it's even necessary
you remind me, as if you could read my thoughts,
it's not but that doesn't change the reality.

Farewell

I practice saying goodbye in the mirror
wonder if my face will betray me
my eyes broken windows
letting everything out that's supposed to stay in
like light, like warmth, like wishes that you weren't leaving.
I try to say it like it doesn't matter, maybe it doesn't matter,
because no words will keep you here,
no love will keep you here.
You must go. I must watch you leave.
This is how the show ends, and I must not forget my line.

Farewell

I write this poem on the days I cannot
forget you are going to leave.

When you say you don't want to leave,
I think you are going to stay,
I conflate the two, make them one
but there is so much space between them
a lifetime could pass by.
You are going to leave.

HEART NOTES

Farewell

Sometimes I imagine the word "go" as a butterfly
fluttering by feelings
and I become the catcher
the net in my hands
with not enough grace
and too short of reach.
It will always find home in you
and I will never capture it.
I should appreciate its beauty instead.

Farewell

When we sat by the river you told me
you were afraid I was running.
Pouring my life into yours would be running
away from a future we both thought best.
You didn't tell me you were the river.
You'd always be running
and I could never keep current.

Farewell

The week I told you I loved you
I started writing your goodbye poem.
Which is to say from that moment I've been trying
to learn how to hold on and let go at the same time.

PARTING GIFT

I want to see you succeed with
all my heart. Wrap it up in a towel,
stuff it in a suitcase, and carry it
with you on your adventures.
Let it lay by your bedside
let it be your alarm clock or
let it be buried beneath
the sound of African drums. At night,
I will not know where you are,
or who you will be with,
but I will feel better knowing my heart
is with you.

MAGNET POEM 5/7

Always
flowers in my heart
make home of our hug
time know us
like a safe secret

SPRING

I waited for spring
                         spring sprang into action
                                            action
feels better under the sun
                    the sun's favorite
action is springing sunshine on strangers
                               strangers don't
know I waited for spring, they thought I was happy
                             I am happy most
when you are with me like in the fall
                         I fell for you in winter
      winter willed itself into beauty and promised a
brighter future

                         a brighter future looked like
you
you looked like the future
                future is as fleeting as spring, always
bright daylight but never lasting

                    never lasting is what you said we were.

HEART NOTES

said all this brightness has to burn out
                                        out there the world is
too big and we are too young
                                          young people love
the hardest though, don't we?
The hardest though is watching spring bloom into a
goodbye
                      Goodbye
            gets stuck in my throat
                           my throat thinks it'd rather
die than let it go
        let go is what spring teaches us
                                  spring teaches
us about the birds and the bees and how they're always
                                                moving
moving is what you are
                you are moving and I am rain
                                I am rain, waiting

to see how you bloom.

BRIGHT

Bright be / fireflies at midnight or / your smile, something to look for in all this darkness. / Bright be / walking outside in the summer, squinting eyes from sunrays or / your heart when you share it with me, all sun in soft palm stretched out to warm me. / Bright be / stained glass kissed by daylight or / your lips pressed to my cheek. / Bright be / the pulsing strobe at your favorite concert or / the beat of your heart. / Bright be / the flashlight during hide and seek or / your spirit, all that wonder wandering.

RITUAL

How do I look
at my favorite face,
watch it twist itself into a lie
call itself ugly
words too familiar on the tongue
stone smoothed by habit.

Everything is a ritual
the mirror, the eating,
the counting, the bathroom.
Do it the same way enough
times and it starts to feel right like praying
to the only god you believe in.

I have my own rituals
look at you as long as
I can without you noticing,
serve you every kind word your heart has
forgotten how to hold down,
guess the number of steps it'll take to get to you
treat it as a New Years' Eve countdown sealed with a kiss,
sit in the bathroom just a minute longer
so I know it's another minute you're not in there.

I call them love rituals.
Do them the same way every
time and it feels right like praying to the only
   god   I believe.

MAGNET POEM 6/7

Care for someone
time makes us
      beautiful and better
we flower together

ON STAYING

It is an unexpected beauty
like discovering water in a desert,
when you're sure it didn't exist,
confident you'd tasted your last drop already
an oasis appears, and you weep
tears you didn't know you had.

When you decide to stay,
I weep tears I didn't know I had
find Santa's present under the tree
the quarter under my pillow
the Easter egg in my basket
I believe in Magic
because I have it in my hands.

When I hold you
I believe in Magic
because I have it in my hands.

Thank God you stayed.

GHOST SHIPS

You love pictures of boats,
their mass of intricacies magnificent and moving
each image a vision of a voyage
not taken, a what if lost
at sea, a lifetime left to the wind.
You wonder what the waves
feel like against that ship,
how that deck creaks,
whether those sails dip.

You do not long for them
anymore, but you appreciate
their beauty and the possibility
of a happiness you will never know.

You are happy now.
This boat is enough.

Wave as the ghost ships pass.

HEART NOTES

BUBBLE TEA HAIKU

Put them together
the messes make more than thought,
like love or magic.

HEART NOTES

EDEN

(quote by Alfred Lord Tennyson)

If I had a flower
for every time I thought
of you I could walk
through my garden
forever

> what a garden that would be,
> filled with all the beauty
> you've shown me.
> Soil the same softness as your spirit
> your daffodil demeanor
> shining like daylight
> your laugh littered like lilacs
> across a garden of goodness.
> I would stand barefoot,
> palms up,
> face to sky,
> and breathe.

MAGNET POEM 7/7

Your love
a kindness always
beautiful with warm
flower feelings
in my heart like home

HEART NOTES

WHAT A BEAUTIFUL WORLD

The earth is 3,958 miles
with 195 countries
that occupy 7 continents
surrounded by 5 oceans.

There is a whole wide world out there
and like fingers through hair
you will comb through all of it
leave no stone unturned
like you and God are playing
hide & seek.

You've already seen more than most
yet your eyes still find mine and
see possibility out of this world.
How did I become a wonder
you want to experience?
It is an ancient mystery
that has no answer, but begs to be known.

You know me.
Like wanderers we stumbled upon each other
on a land unfamiliar yet made a home
out of sticks and stones and smiles and the unknown
and you stayed.

So when you travel miles
visit countries,
touch continents,
sail oceans

HEART NOTES

you always find
your way back and my heart
is the happiest home.

HEART NOTES

ACKNOWLEDGEMENTS

Thank you, Maggie. You've shown me a type of love I've never known, and without it, I wouldn't be who I am today. This book is as much yours as it is mine, because this is my heart in its truest form. I give it to you.

Thank you Joanne and George for being the first ones to show me love and for being the ones I can depend on to love me through it all.

Thank you to Keegan Gormally for being such an amazing editor and an even better person. The kind of goodness you hold is rare and beautiful.

Thank you to Ophelia Flores-Carr for creating such a beautiful cover. You've made my heart happy.

Thank you to Liz, Allison, Lindley, Mahogany, Rachael, and Laurie for sharing your hearts with me. We were never perfect, but we did grow, and that is all we can ever really ask for.

Thank you to Jared, Ellis, Alec, Solomon, and Venson for being the kind of friends that help me unpack my own heart—it gets cluttered and heavy and you all help me see through it all when I need it most.

Thank you to everyone who has shown me support up until this point. I am the result of all the love I've been given by you. Thank you, thank you, thank you.

ABOUT THE AUTHOR

Caleb "The Negro Artist" Rainey is an author, performer, and producer. He hails from Columbia, Missouri, and holds a bachelors degree in English (Creative Writing) from the University of Iowa. His debut book, Look, Black Boy, became Amazon's #1 new release in African American poetry, and was featured on Iowa Public Radio. He co-founded the literary magazine Black Art; Real Stories, has been published in the Little Village Magazine, and writes a monthly column in The Real Mainstream.

As a performer he is the winner of the Des Moines Poetry Slam, the Iowa City Poetry Slam, a two-time winner of the Fire & Ice Poetry Slam, and a finalist for the UNESCO City of Literature Global Poetry Slam – Iowa City. He has done spoken word across the nation including Iowa, Missouri, Nebraska, Wisconsin, Indiana, Colorado, Illinois, New York City, and has even performed internationally in London, England. He was the opening poet for Dan Brown, featured on the album *Blk Boi Joy*, and acted in the Iowa debut of the plays, *Exit Strategy* and *Luna Gale*.

When he is not writing and performing he is actively curating a community of spoken word poets in Iowa City through his creation of a high school workshop program, IC Speaks, and producing local events like Poetry & Motion.

HEART NOTES